I0405368

Agile For All

Managing Any Project Like
A Silicon Valley Startup

Richard Bryan Vaughn

*To Armand, who pushes me to be the best
that I can be.*

Chapter 1:

Introduction to Agile

Hello, Project Manager. Welcome, come in! Congratulations on taking the first step towards guiding your company's projects from the rigid, stodgy methods of the twentieth century to the adaptable, agile methods of the twenty-first. I know that things will seem a little bit strange here at first, but don't worry. I'm here to help you out until you get used to it. This book will guide you through the ins and outs, over the pitfalls, and around the challenges of introducing Agile Project Management into any company and with any project type.

First, let's talk about what is Agile Project Management, or just "Agile." Agile, also sometimes called "Scrum" because of its similarity with the way a rugby team's members pass the ball between them as they run down the field, was born in the software development world and has been widely used since the early 2000s. Agile was developed by software teams whose members had spent their careers under a "waterfall" system, with business requirements crashing down on them from above and their final deliverables flowing away from them, downriver, never to be seen again. They wanted to devise a system that allowed them to be flexible, have greater visibility to the overall scope of their projects, and to be nimble enough to react to frequently changing requirements… to be "agile," if you will. With these goals in mind, Agile software development was born.

If you ask any software developers today, they will tell you that Agile is the pervasive project management system throughout the industry. They will tell you how great it is, how much independence it gives them, and they will praise those who developed it as visionaries in the industry. Dig a little deeper, though, and you'll learn something interesting. Go visit some software developers and ask them about Agile, but when they're off playing ping-pong or taking a company-sponsored yoga break find their project managers. Ask the project managers about Agile and you will hear something like, "Yeah, we kind of use Agile, but we don't follow it exactly," or, "We started out trying to follow Agile, but it has evolved over time. Now it's more like an Agile-lite." At first this might be alarming to you. If Agile is so great, why would no one be following it properly? Why is everyone changing the rules? Well, the reason for this is right there in front of you: *Agile is agile.* By its very nature the process wants to be flexible, open to changing as new requirements and priorities come along. This is good news for you, because it is this very adaptability of Agile that allows us to tweak and twist it a in order to work with any project type, anywhere. Keeping the foundation in place, we can drop out the details that are required only for software development and expand our language to work in any business environment.

So, what are those foundations that we need to maintain? I have boiled them down into six easy rules that we always need to follow to remain agile. Beyond these, you can feel free to explore and modify the process to work with your own teams. These rules are:

1. Projects always have a defined goal.
2. Every project team has at least one member dedicated to the project.
3. Every team representative is involved throughout the entire length of the project.
4. Individuals, not groups, own responsibility for project tasks.
5. All sprint deliverables must be demoed at the review meeting.
6. Projects must be broken up into equal sprints of time, capped on each end by a review meeting.

This may be a bit confusing, so before we dive into the nitty-gritty of setting up a project using Agile, let's explore each of these rules in a bit of detail.

1. *Projects always have a defined goal.* Put another way: every project must have a clearly defined end point that everyone agrees to at the start of the project. This isn't to say that you need to know at the beginning of the project exactly what that final product will look like, but it does mean that you do need to be able to say, "When this project is over, we will have accomplished X." This means that the task deliverables assigned to this project may only be geared towards getting to accomplishment X. If, midway through the project, it is decided that you also need to work on accomplishments Y and Z, then those accomplishments need to have their own projects built around them. Once accomplishment X is completed, if the

company decides that you now need to meet accomplishment X-version 2, then the first project ends and a new one may be launched.

2. *Every project team has at least one member dedicated to the project.* Depending on the nature of your business these teams will be different, but in general think of a "team" as a group of people, probably in the same department, who work within the same discipline. Legal, finance, graphic design, PR, media development, operations, sales… all of these could be considered "teams." Any team that is going to have any impact on the project *must* have at least one person dedicated to the project from beginning to end. A project may not start until each team has assigned their dedicated representative to it.

3. *Every team representative is involved throughout the entire length of the project.* No matter how long a project is

and how early or late in the project a team may be the most active, the representative of must be involved in the project from beginning to end. During some periods this involvement may only be participating in a biweekly project meeting, but the involvement must be there nonetheless. In this way, every team has visibility into the scope and progression of the project, allowing them to both plan their work well ahead of its delivery and to add valuable feedback at the earliest possible stage in the project.

4. *Individuals, not groups, own responsibility for project tasks.* If you assign tasks to a particular team rather than an individual on that team, you will always run into the risk of having a table full of people looking at each other with "it wasn't my job to get that done" looks on their faces when the time comes to present on that deliverable. When tasks are being assigned, they must always be assigned to an individual, whose job it

then is to bring together any resources that he or she needs in order to accomplish that task.

5. *All sprint deliverables must be demoed at the review meeting.* As you work towards the project accomplishment, many various pieces are going to have to come together like the pieces of jigsaw puzzle. Can you imagine trying to put together a puzzle without being able to look at all the pieces? Of course not. Different teams working on disparate parts of the project can benefit not only in their own work by tangibly seeing what others are working on, but letting different groups comment on work by every other team can give a fresh perspective to a task that narrow attention by only one discipline can't provide.

6. *Projects must be broken up into generally equal sprints of time, capped on each end by a review meeting.* The Sprint (a period of time) and the Sprint

Review (a meeting at the end of each Sprint) are among the most important features of Agile. At the beginning of each project it is your job to determine how long each Sprint in the upcoming project will be. Typically two-week Sprints are normal, but in tighter or longer projects shorter or longer sprints may be acceptable. At the beginning/end of each Sprint there is a Sprint Review meeting where the representatives of each team must attend. In short, the agenda of every Sprint Review is a) a demo of all of the accomplishments from the ending Sprint then b) planning the deliverables for the next Sprint.

This is all pretty simple so far, right? Great. From here on out, everything that we will cover will be details on how you can set up projects following these rules for yourself. First we'll talk about how you can introduce Agile to your organization to get the approval you'll need to make what may be a drastic switch in process and buy-in from the stakeholders who will be participants in your future projects. After that, we'll talk about how to get started setting up a new project with Agile. Then we will cover how to run an ongoing project, from the meetings you'll be running to tricks to keeping a project on track. We will also discuss common pitfalls that project managers can have and how to address them. Finally, we'll discuss wrapping up a project and delivery of your accomplishments. By the end of this book you will have everything you need to introduce Agile Project Management in any organization.

Chapter 2:

Laying the Groundwork

The first step that you need in order to introduce Agile into your organization is a solid foundation. To begin building this foundation, let's first develop some common definitions for the terms that we'll be using.

Sprint- A Sprint is a period of time during which team members agree to a defined set of tasks that will be demoed at the end of the Sprint. At the beginning of each project you need to decide how long you want each Sprint to be, and once you decide on this all the Sprints in the project should be the same length. Two weeks is typical, though in shorter projects one-week Sprints are acceptable. The Sprint is capped at either end by a Sprint Review meeting.

Sprint Review- The Sprint Review is the most important meeting in the Agile universe. Scheduled at the end of each Sprint period, the Sprint Review is the time when all of the project team members come together, review and demo all of the work that was done in the previous Sprint, and plan out what work will be done in the upcoming Sprint.

Task- A Task, or Deliverable, is a piece of work large enough that it can be shown in demo-able form, but not so large that one person can't be held responsible for its completion. Multiple people may be called on to work on a Task, but there should always be one person who is primarily responsible to see that it gets done. For example, creating a single presentation slide is too small to be a task. Developing an entirely new sales process is too large. Building a presentation about a new sales process is just the right size that it can be managed by one person and delivered in a single Sprint.

Demo- The first part of the Sprint Review meeting is dedicated to demoing the Tasks that were accomplished during the last Sprint. In this case, "Demo" is not just a euphemism for talking about the work that was done. It means physically showing- up on a screen or tangibly in front of you- the work that was done and eliciting feedback from the project team members on it. The Demo is important because it allows everyone on the project to see how all the other project components are shaping up and to give feedback from their various points-of-view.

Backlog- The Backlog is the list of Tasks that are required to complete the project. At the beginning of the project it is helpful to make a list of all of the Tasks that you know will be necessary to complete it, however there is no rule that you can't add new Tasks to the project backlog over time as you figure them out *so long as they relate to completing the designated accomplishments for this project.* If a good idea comes along related to the thing you're working on, but not directly to the project at hand, you can put it in a

Backlog for the product or service as a whole to be addressed in a later project.

Now that we have some of the terminology established, let's talk about why Agile is good for you as a project manager and why it will be good for your company. Projects are considered most successful when they are delivered on time and on budget, right? Well, what are the main reasons that you may miss your deadlines or go over budget? The most obvious answer is that you miss deadlines when the different pieces of the project take longer to deliver than was originally estimated. There can be many factors explaining why project components take longer to deliver than expected, but they all boil down to a lack of communication. When different teams on the project don't communicate regularly they can lose track of progress being made elsewhere, develop different pieces that won't integrate properly, and not get changes in requirements until work has already been done, making it necessary to backtrack and redo effort. Agile is designed to solve this communication problem. By having regular, structured check-ins with all stakeholders and participants, the lines of communication are kept open for information to flow freely and quickly throughout the entire project team.

You may now be well convinced that Agile is right for your company, but depending on the size, structure, and culture of your organization, getting the ball rolling on implementing Agile may not be easy. Since it will be new to you, as the project manager, as well as everyone else, I recommend that you suggest trying it out in just one small, self-contained project. This will allow you to get your feet wet without too much risk. It will also earn you some converts, as the members of that project will see how streamlined and efficient it can be. They will make good allies for you when pitching your case to spread Agile further to upper management.

To help get you started, I have prepared a couple of email templates that you can use. First, you will likely need to get approval to switch to a whole new project management system. Use this template for an email to kick-off the conversation with your boss or whoever needs to approve the switch:

Dear _____,

As you know, our team has been following the same type of structure for our project management for some time now. While it has generally been working fine, I have been reading up on new, more modern methods for project management and I would like to propose that we begin to explore ways to improve our process.

In the software development world, a process called Agile has been evolving for the last decade, and I think that implementing a modified form of this methodology suited to our industry will help our teams be more efficient and productive. Agile developed around the need to be nimble and able to react quickly to a fast-changing environment, and I believe that adopting it will allow us to turn out more deliverables more quickly, with less time spent on backtracking or revising plans.

For a first step, I propose that we identify a small, non-critical project where I can take the lead on implementing Agile. This project can be used as a proof-of-concept for our company and to identify any changes that may need to be made to the process before rolling it out to the rest of the organization.

I would be happy to meet with you as soon as it is convenient to discuss the

*new process I am proposing in detail and
to begin work on identifying a test
project.*

Best Regards,

_____

There are a couple of things that
you may notice about this first template:
First, I gave a brief overview of the high-
level benefits of Agile, but did not go
into great detail. When seeking
approval, you will likely need to
emphasize just two main things: that it is
an established process and the benefits it
will bring to your teams and the
company. You may have the kind of
boss who wants to know all of the nitty-
gritty details about how this process will
work, so always make sure that you are

willing and ready to discuss them, but don't try to put it all into an introductory email. This will be too overwhelming and you will get blocked from making any changes before you even get started. Second, notice that I emphasized the fact that I (you) will be taking responsibility for owning the testing and implementation of this new process. You are going out of your way to learn about Agile just by reading this book, so I know that you are the kind of person who wants to drive their own career forward. Take this as an opportunity to demonstrate your leadership to your boss and teammates. Own the process, and when Agile is successfully implemented you will become the go-to expert on project management for your company.

This next email template is for your colleagues on the test project once it has been approved to introduce them to the new process. I recommend that you start out by identifying the team leads who will be responsible for their groups on the project. Then, send them this email to lay out the plan and make them feel comfortable with the new process that they will be part of.

Hi everyone!

You are all on this email because you will be team leads on the upcoming _____ project. I am sending this email to let you know about a new project management process called Agile that we will be testing out during the course of this project.

For those who aren't familiar with it, Agile is a project management methodology out of Silicon Valley that focuses on work getting done in two-week Sprints. At the beginning of each Sprint I will be scheduling a Sprint Review meeting. The purpose of this meeting is to demo the work that was done in the previous Sprint and to plan the work for the upcoming Sprint. As team leads, you will each be individually responsible for making sure that the work you commit to for your team gets done and for demoing it at each Sprint Review meeting.

In the beginning, I know that not all of your teams will be actively doing work on this project; some of you have involvement that gets heavier near the end. This is understood, but I would like to emphasize now that it is important for all team leads, regardless of what they're delivering on during that Sprint, show up to and participate in every Sprint Review. The Sprint Reviews are the time for all of us to provide feedback on the work everyone else has done and to raise concerns if work being done now will affect something further down the line.

As a first step, I will be scheduling a Project Kick Off meeting where we will *review the project deliverables, any work that has already been done on them, and plan the deliverables for the first Sprint.*

If you have any questions, please feel free to let me know. Additionally, since this is a pilot in our company for the Agile process, please let me know throughout the project if you see any room for improvement.

Best Regards,

_____

Now, what was different about this template from the one above? First, it was more concrete in its description of what Agile is. This email is targeted towards the people who will be participating day-to-day in the process, so they will want to know details of what they are being brought into. Second, we are emphasizing right off the bat the notion of individual responsibility in Agile. In the past we may have had dispersed team responsibility for deliverables, so this new notion of calling on a single person to own a deliverable may encounter some resistance. As the project manager and owner of this new process, it will be up to you to sell the value of individual task ownership to your entire team. Finally, you will notice that we want to invite as much feedback on the process as possible. Most of Agile is not written in stone, so you will want to evolve it to work best with your organization. The best way to do this is to understand what is working for your teammates and what they would like to see improvement on.

Unfortunately, as we have all learned at one time or another, people can be resistant to change, so they need some strong arguments to convince them to give up the status quo. At the face of it, Agile can seem like an intensive process- lots of meetings, rigid structure, taking up the time of people who won't be involved in the project until later... When introducing the concept to your management and your teams, you are going to need to have answers to these types of questions ready. Since Agile is new to you, I have prepared a cheat-sheet of talking points that will help you win over even your most entrenched team members.

Why do we need to change? Our current process is fine. Management theories are constantly evolving and any process that has been settled for more than a few years is likely out-of-date. We want to make sure that our company is on the cutting edge in everything we do to stay ahead of our competitors. Agile grew up over the last ten years in the software development world where it was tested and refined. The fast-paced world of software development means that any process born there will focus on efficiency, speed, and quality, all of which are things that are important to us too.

It seems like there are an awfully lot of meetings. The only meetings that all the project team members are required to attend are the Sprint Reviews, which only happen every two weeks. In between those, team members are assigned tasks to work on. To complete those tasks, they may need to call meetings with the relevant stakeholders, but those will always be targeted meetings just for getting the work on that task done.

My team doesn't need to be involved until the end of the project. Why should I have to attend meetings before then? Do you remember how in every other project you got involved near the end, saw the almost-complete project goal, and said, "This part shouldn't be done this way! I wish I had seen this sooner to tell you."

Well, here is your chance to see it sooner and tell everyone. Even if you don't have specific task deliverables during a Sprint, during the demo portion of the Sprint Review you will be able to see what other groups are working on and comment on them well before they get to you. In addition to that, you will also be able to see what work is coming your way further down the line so that you and your team can prepare for it.

I like to be able to see a perfectly laid-out schedule of the project from beginning-to-end. "Agile" sounds a little too uncertain to me. How often has your project ever perfectly followed the schedule that was laid out for it on Day 1? Probably never. New requirements, unforeseen circumstances or changes, and unexpected challenges always waylay the best-laid schedules. Agile allows you to look forward in manageable chunks of time. You can always set a project completion deadline-

and it is the job of the project manager to make sure that you stay on track to hit it- but the majority of the project team members will only need to be worried about concrete deliverables for two weeks out.

My team doesn't work with responsibility handed to just one person. We don't want tasks assigned to an individual because we always work as a collective group. Assigning a task to an individual doesn't mean that this person must take on all the work his- or herself. It means that this person is responsible for marshalling whatever resources are necessary to complete the task during the sprint, for presenting the demo of the task at the Sprint Review, and ultimately for making sure that the task is completed on time. If a task is assigned to a group as a whole and then it is not complete when the time comes to deliver on it, it's too easy for everyone in the group to shrug their shoulders, point their fingers, and say, "it wasn't my job to see that it got done."

What if Agile just doesn't work for us? The beauty of Agile is that it is "agile." No two companies use it in exactly the same way. At the end of every project, there should be a time when the project manager asks everyone to look back and think about what could have been done differently to improve the process. We will take this feedback and incorporate it going forward so that Agile works at its best for our company.

You may have to go through a few layers of management in order to get final approval to run a project as an Agile pilot. Don't get discouraged if this process takes a little time. The more entrenched the old system is, the more people will be resistant to change it. If you keep pushing, though, you will find that the older and more burdensome the old process was, the more successful the change to Agile will be.

Chapter 3:

Starting Your First Project

Now that you have gotten approval for your test project you are ready to get everything set up. Starting your first project involves four steps:

1. Choosing a task management tool.
2. Doing your pre-project task set up.
3. Determining the team members who will be on your project.
4. Kicking off with a Project Initiation meeting.

Choosing a task management tool.

At the beginning of your first Agile project, you are going to want to choose a method of organizing your tasks. If you don't already have a tool that you like and use regularly, I recommend finding an online tool to manage your tasks. Online, cloud-based tools allow anyone on the team to view all the project deliverables at any time. There are many different online tools that you may want to choose from to make your organization easier, ranging in complexity and fullness of functionality. The key that you want to look for is a tool that allows you to assign, edit, and move tasks easily. You also want something that will allow you to organize your tasks into clearly distinguishable Sprint groups. Here are a few options that I recommend, but you can feel free to explore for others:

JIRA- Created by Atlassian, JIRA is a tool designed for Agile management of software development. (www.atlassian.com/software/jira)

Pros:

- Designed with Agile in mind. Easy to set up and track Sprints and Backlogs.
- Extremely robust functionality.
- Infinitely customizable.
- Decent reporting.

Cons:

- Can be very complex to set up and use.
- High learning curve that may dissuade new users.

Asana with Instagantt- Asana is an online task-management tool. Instagantt is a separate tool that pulls in data from Asana to display it on a Gantt chart. (www.asana.com and www.instagantt.com)

Pros:

- Easy to set up with a low learning curve for new team members.
- Easy to view project timelines.
- Set up different Teams with different members so sensitive projects can be hidden from those who shouldn't see them.

Cons:

- Since Asana alone doesn't have the concept of a task start date (just a due date) or show Gantt charting, you need two separate tools to get this functionality.
- Not designed with Agile in mind, so you need some creative use of sub-headings and labels to indicate different Sprints or Backlog tasks.
- Minimal reporting.

Trello- Trello is an online task management tool that allows you to maintain a list of ideas and track their progress. (www.trello.com)

Pros:

- Maintain all of your tasks on an easy to read board.

- Manage the project across multiple device platforms.

Cons:

- No clear way to divide work up into Sprints.
- No overall project timeline views.

Doing your pre-project task set up.

Once you have selected a task management tool to use, you will want to work to identify all of the tasks that you already know and get them recorded in the tool.

In traditional Agile, software development tasks are divided up as "Stories" and "Sub-Tasks." A Story is a piece of functionality based on something that will be used by somebody. For example, "As a website user, I would like a login page to enter my username and password." Many different people or teams may be involved in the different pieces of a Story, so it is then broken down into Sub-Tasks, which are small pieces of work assigned to one individual. Examples of Sub-Tasks for this Story may be: Marketing designs for the login page; create database to store member login information; front end code development of login page; etc.

Since you don't necessarily create software products you may not want to follow this exact format, but you may find it useful to think about your deliverables in this manner: a large piece broken down into different component pieces. For example, if your Story was to create a slide deck for a new product, your subtasks may be: product development provides details of new product; marketing provides new slide templates; source images of new project; copy editing reviews content on deck; etc.

No matter how you decide to break up your tasks, before the project kickoff you should try to identify as many deliverables as possible. Keep in mind, though, that you will often not know all of the component deliverables from the start. It will be the responsibility of the team leads throughout the project to identify the work their teams need to do in order to reach your end goals.

Along with the tasks and deliverables that you are able to identify, before the project kickoff you should also gather together any documentation or work that has already been done towards this project's deliverables. This may include requirements that have already been written up, preliminary designs, a previous version or iteration of something that is being updated, or anything else that already exists that will guide this project. At the kickoff you want to be prepared to present on all of these to the rest of the team, so make sure that you are fully comfortable with them before that meeting.

Determining the team members who will be on your project.

The first step to determining who needs to be on your project team is to determine what groups or departments need to be represented. Does your project have design work that will require Marketing? Is it a new product that Sales will have to weigh in on? Once you determine all of the teams that will need to be represented in this project, then you can go through your company's process for finding the specific individuals who will be on your project for its duration. Depending on the amount of work each team will be expected to contribute, it may be necessary to have more than one representative from some teams on your project. However, don't forgot that you are always assigning tasks to individuals, not to multiple people or entire teams, and that it is the responsibility of those individuals to bring together the necessary resources to complete their tasks.

Once you have identified the teams that need to work on your project and the individual people who will represent those teams to your projects, then you are ready to reach out and introduce Agile to them. In Chapter 2 I provided an email template that you may find helpful to establish the new process that you will be using and to answer questions that you colleagues will have on starting with a new process.

Kicking off with a Project Initiation meeting.

Now that you have identified your team leads, gotten them up to speed on the new Agile process, and done your pre-project set-up, you are ready to schedule your Project Initiation Meeting. You can think of the Project Initiation Meeting as your first Sprint Review. Depending on the size of the project, you will likely want to schedule at least one hour for this meeting. At this meeting you will be setting the tone for all future Sprint Reviews, so there are a few things you want to make sure get established here:

- All teams must have at least one representative present. The success of Agile, and therefore your project, depends on participation by all groups throughout the entirety of the project, so make sure that this is communicated clearly and often.
- Everyone with a deliverable must be prepared to present that deliverable in a demo. Establish this precedent by

being thoroughly prepared to share the documentation that already exists for the project that you identified in your pre-project analysis.

- As the project manager, you are ultimately in charge of all Sprint meetings. You need to take the lead right off the bat in setting the agenda and keeping everyone to it. Strong leadership will help the meetings be more efficient, and with efficiency participants who may have otherwise been skeptical will see the value in the Agile process.

- Strike the right balance between discussion and moving the meeting along. Participants are encouraged to provide feedback to other members throughout the entire length of the project, so you want to make sure that you allow time with each demo for participate and feedback. However, if the feedback starts to become too conversational or to delve too deeply into one particular subject, you must use your leadership to cut the conversation off and move the meeting along. If there is a valuable discussion on a deliverable that ought to be continued, set a Sprint Goal to follow up on the item and resolve it and assign someone to be responsible for managing this.

As with any important meeting, ahead of it you will want to publish an agenda. Here is a sample for the Project Initiation Meeting:

1. Introduction
   a. Introduce the project and its ultimate deliverable.
   b. Brief overview of the Agile process that will be used. If this is a pilot program with Agile, explain that it is and give a way for participants to provide feedback.
   c. Establish Sprint and meeting cadence (two-week Sprints with Sprint Reviews capping

them on the same day every
other week).

2. Demo
   a. Show on a shared screen all of
      the documentation,
      requirements, etc. that were
      gathered during the pre-project
      review.
   b. Walk through each document,
      encouraging feedback from
      the participants.

3. Set Sprint Goals
   a. Present the assumed Sprint
      Goals that you developed
      during the pre-project review
      *and get agreement from each
      of the people responsible that
      they will be able to deliver on
      those goals in the next Sprint.*
      If the task assignee does not
      believe that the goal is
      attainable (or necessary), then
      strike it from the list.
   b. Go around the table to every
      team lead and ask them what,

if anything, they plan on being able to accomplish in the next Sprint. If they say they have nothing, but you think that there are deliverables they ought to be working towards, you can suggest deliverables for them to consider. For a first Sprint, these deliverables may be as simple as doing due diligence on the project requirements to present back a project plan or project deliverables list for their team. *Note: Not all people or teams may have deliverables for the first Sprint; however, you want to make sure to give everyone the opportunity to speak up because they may know deliverables their teams will need to work towards that you don't have the visibility to in order to have thought of ahead of time.*

4. Closing
   a. Open up the floor to any final comments or feedback.
   b. Remind everyone of the next Sprint Review's date and time, and that these meetings will be every two week (or whatever your cadence is) until the end of the project.

After the Project Initiation Meeting, you will want to finalize it by publishing the recording of the meeting and sending out a link to it to all invitees and by publishing the meeting notes and deliverables. Personally, I like to update the calendar invitation for the next Sprint Review right away with the deliverables for that sprint. This gives everyone the same written record of what was decided upon so there can be no excuses at the next Sprint Review that someone didn't know what was assigned to them. Ahead of a Sprint Review, the agenda template that I like to put into the calendar invitation looks something like this:

Agenda

1. Sprint Overview
   a. Sprint Dates: March 1 – March 14
   b. High-Level Update
2. Demo of Deliverables
   a. Team A
       i. Deliverable 1 (John)
       ii. Deliverable 2 (John)
   b. Team B
       i. Deliverable 1 (Samantha)
   c. Team C
       i. *No deliverables*
   d. Team D
       i. Deliverable 1 (Ben)
       ii. Deliverable 2 (Tami)
3. Sprint Planning
   a. Team A
   b. Team B

    c. Team C

    d. Team D

4. Wrap Up

    a. Next Sprint: March 15 - March 28

    b. Final Feedback

Chapter 4:

Running a Project

At this point, you have learned about Agile, convinced your company to let you run a trial project, set up your pilot, and kicked it off with a Project Initiation Meeting. Now what? Now your project is up and running and you can settle into a regular cadence. Every two weeks you will have a Sprint Review meeting where all your team leads (or their representatives) will come together to review and provide feedback on deliverables and plan out the next Sprint. This process will continue until your project is complete. As an Agile project manager, your role is more hands-on than it might be under other project management methodologies. This means that you don't just have a Sprint Review and let everyone go off on their merry way, not checking in with them at all for two weeks. A successful project manager will make sure to keep abreast of everything going on in the project. With a complete picture of what everyone is doing, you will not only be able to see dependencies and how one team's work might affect another's, but you will also be able to play an intelligent role in providing deliverable feedback and recommendations for deliverables in upcoming Sprints to the various teams.

After you have run your Project Initiation Meeting, the process for running Sprint Reviews will be familiar. As discussed at the end of the previous chapter, after the Project Initiation you will want to publish the agenda for the upcoming Sprint Review, including all agreed-upon deliverables and their assigned owners. When the time comes for the Sprint Review meeting, don't forget to keep these points in mind:

- Always record the meetings and publish the recording for any invitees who weren't able to attend.
- As the project manager, take leadership and ownership. It is your

job and nobody else's to keep the meetings on topic and on track.

- All deliverables have specific individuals assigned to them, so don't be afraid to call people out by name to demo. Everyone with tasks to deliver should always come to Sprint Reviews prepared to demo.

- Be prepared to be an active participant in the conversation by keeping up with all work being done on the project. In providing feedback to deliverables, your voice is just as important as any other team member's.

- You are a part of the team, just the same as every other member. You are not above, outside, or different from the other team leads. Just like all the others, you have responsibilities to meet for each Sprint and are a part of the effort in moving everyone towards the final goal.

The agenda for a standard Sprint Review will be similar to the Project Initiation, with just some minor changes once everyone gets into the rhythm of the process:

1. Introduction and Sprint Overview
    a. Give a high-level overview of the project's current state. This may include things like:
        i.   How close you are getting to any important deadlines.
        ii. If you are on track, ahead of schedule, or behind schedule.
        iii. Any notable changes that have been made in the direction of the project.
        iv. Any big accomplishments made worth celebrating.
        v.   Any changes to project membership (team lead

> change of
> responsibilities,
> addition of new
> members to a team,
> etc.).

2. Demo of Deliverables
    a. Unlike during the Project
       Initiation Meeting, you should
       not be the primary presenter
       during this portion in regular
       Sprint Reviews. You should
       be able to hand control of the
       meeting and any screen-
       sharing to the person
       responsible for delivering and
       demoing each task.
    b. As much as possible, follow
       the established order of
       deliverables in the published
       agenda. This will help prevent
       people from getting caught
       off-guard when you ask them
       to present.
    c. If someone is unable to demo
       because their deliverable isn't

ready, you need to find out why the task wasn't completed and when it can be expected. Make sure that you strike the balance between being firm and helpful, without being accusatory or setting a confrontational tone. For the assignee that missed a deliverable deadline, the experience should be uncomfortable enough that they don't want to repeat it, but should never be unpleasant. Above all else, you need to make sure in this circumstance that you are focused on moving the project forward from today, looking back only to learn from the past to not repeat any mistakes that may have been made.

d. It is important to allow time for team members to provide feedback on every item that is demoed, however you will often find that people will want to have in-depth discussions. Once you identify a discussion starting that seems like it will take longer than two or three minutes, feel free to jump in and stop the conversation. Point out the importance of the topic, that it deserves a longer conversation than the format of this meeting will allow, and offer to set up a follow-up meeting with the appropriate subset of people.

3. Sprint Planning
   a. With your knowledge of all the work being done in the project, the expected future deliverables, and the timelines, you can plan ahead to have some deliverables ready to recommend to the team leads for the next Sprint.

b. Always make sure to give each team lead or representative the opportunity to offer deliverables for their team. Call on each one individually to make sure that they either offer up their planned work or actively say that they have nothing that needs to be done during this Sprint.

c. You will likely find it helpful during the demos to keep notes on tasks brought up then that should be accomplished in the next Sprint. During demos there will often be feedback provided to incorporate or next steps discussed that will become Sprint Goals for the upcoming Sprint.

4. Wrap Up

a. Always open the floor one last time for anyone to bring up any issues or comments that

they did not have the
opportunity to bring up before.
b. Emphasize any immediate
action items that came up
during the meeting, including
follow-up on any discussion
that you had to cut short in the
interest of time.
c. Especially during your earlier
Sprints and projects, offer up
the opportunity, either here or
separately, for participants to
provide you feedback on the
meetings and the project
management process.

As far as being a project manager
on an Agile project goes, these are
essentially all of the tools that you will
need to manage a project. You may
want to modify some portions, such as
meeting agendas, to meet your own
needs, but this foundation will support
you no matter what shape your Agile
structure takes. To go beyond being just

the project manager to be a team member and a team leader, though, there are a number of areas that I suggest you focus on. These will allow you to not only manage projects more effectively, but to show your leadership skills to the wide cross-section of the company that will interact with your projects.

First and foremost, make sure that your attitude and approach are that of a team member, in the trenches working on the tasks of the projects with everyone else, and not as an outsider just responsible for coordinating other people. Remember the alternative name for Agile that we discussed in Chapter 1- Scrum- which evokes the image of a rugby team all working together to get a ball down the field. You can do this in a variety of ways:

- Take the time and spend the effort to learn about all of the component deliverables to your project. If the project is in a field that you haven't worked much in before, do some research or seek out other project managers who have worked in that field to understand the pieces that typically need to be included. If you are familiar with the project field, make sure you thoroughly understand the end goal.

- Understand the role of your project in the greater business plan. Knowing well the actual project deliverable and its importance to your business will help you to guide the team members to deliver an appropriate result.

- Get to know everyone on the team. In large organizations or on teams with remote participants, it can be easy to know people just as disembodied voices. If you are physically in the same location as your team members, make an effort to spend time with them to get to know their personalities. If they are remote, find reasons to talk to them one-on-one about project deliverables. Even talking just about the project can help you to better understand how they think and act. Invariably you will find, especially on larger projects, more complex projects, or projects with tougher deadlines that can cause stress within the team, that there will be personality conflicts among different team members. As a leader within the team, you will be better suited to help smooth over these issues if you know the players personally.

- Make an effort to be available to assist team members who are struggling to meet their deliverable deadlines. Although you won't be an expert in every field represented on your team, there will often be ways that you can assist your teammates beyond the normal project manager roles of coordinating and getting questions answered for people. Never allow yourself to think,

"That's not my job;" rather, always keep the image of moving the ball down the field together in mind and ask, "What can I do to help you meet that goal?"

Another way to go above and beyond in your role as a project leader is to learn enough about the day-to-day work of the various team disciplines on your project to be able to talk intelligently with them about their work. For example, if you are working with software developers you don't need to go out and get a degree in computer science, but you should conceptually understand server-side development versus client-side development, what a database is, and what code looks like. If you are working with graphic designers, comfortably managing files in Photoshop shouldn't be a requirement for you, but knowing what a vector graphic is, the differences between a .jpg, .png, and.bmp, and the distinction between flat versus layered files will allow you to effectively understand their deliverables and what they need to produce them.

With this knowledge and these relationships, you will be more productive both as a project manager and as a team leader. During your Sprints, between the Sprint Reviews, the responsibility to accomplish deliverable tasks will ultimately fall on those the deliverables are assigned to. However, as an informed team member you can be a much more active participant in your projects. Check in with the team leaders on their progress midway through the Sprint to make sure that they are going to meet their delivery goals. If it looks like they might not, offer to help yourself or to bring together the appropriate people help them get done. If someone is responsible for a number of deliverables that require the input of other people, offer to help by doing some mini-project management of those deliverables.

Oftentimes you will find that people become team leaders because of their technical expertise in their field, not necessarily because of their skills at managing other people to deliver goals on deadlines. Part of your role needs to be able to identify these issues, understand them, and take steps to solve for them.

Overall, you will find that one of the most important things you can do as an Agile project manager between Sprint Reviews is to make yourself available to your team members. They will always need help with gathering information and resolving dependencies they have on other teams, so your bird's eye knowledge about the entire project and understanding of how the different disciplines function will enable to you easily facilities getting these issues resolved. Often when someone is slipping and in danger of not meeting a Sprint Goal all they need to get back on track is an extra pair of hands. Whether this is you or you are help to help find someone, your ability to identify and solve for this problem will be invaluable.

Chapter 5:

Wrapping Up a Project

When you were setting up your first project, you identified a goal that the project was built around working towards. Throughout the course of the project, you defined the concrete deliverables that would allow you to meet that goal. Now that the project is ending, you must keep in mind that this project is officially over once this goal has been met and those deliverables produced.

During a project you and your team will undoubtedly have ideas about ways in which the project might be extended, the goals expounded upon, and the timelines extended. You must fight back against this scope creep by capturing all of these good ideas and putting them into the Backlog for the product or service that you are working on. If the ideas are good and the business decides to move forward with them, then you can launch a new project with new requirements to work on them, but for each specific project you must be vigilant about meeting just the goals defined and approved for that project.

Back when we were building our foundations in Agile in Chapter 1, we laid out six rules that must always be followed to maintain Agile project management:

1. Projects always have a defined goal.
2. Every project team has at least one member dedicated to the project.
3. Every team representative is involved throughout the entire length of the project.
4. Individuals, not groups, own responsibility for project tasks.
5. All sprint deliverables must be demoed at the review meeting.
6. Projects must be broken up into equal sprints of time, capped on each end by a review meeting.

These rules are the pillars of Agile project management. Beyond them, you may feel free to expand, evolve, and experiment with the process to make it work in your organization. Since Agile was developed in the software development world, when teams of coders use Agile they have a number of additional steps they follow that may not make sense for your organization or project types. Thankfully, Agile being agile, you are not required to use them to follow the methodology. As Agile expands further out from Silicon Valley, more teams adopting it will find new and better ways to use it. Don't be afraid to test and change the way you use the process as you learn more about it and as it expands further in your company.

Ultimately, the purpose of Agile is not to provide just another set of rules into the canon of project manager techniques. Rather, it has evolved from the ground up to help collaborative teams be the most effective, with just enough process to support, but not burden, them.

As the project manager, your job is to be the center lynchpin of this collaboration. Meetings are important tools that you can use to foster this collaboration, but ultimately the best project managers are those who enable their teammates to do their jobs to the maximum of their potential. Being an active member of your team instead of just an outside coordinator will allow you to best provide this support and establish yourself as a strong leader and a great manager of projects.

With this, Project Manager, the time has come for me to say good-bye and let you take this knowledge out with you into the world. You are now able to introduce Agile in your organization, whatever field you might be in. You can take the process from beginning to end and successfully complete your first project. From there you can evolve the process for your organization, and in so doing establish your own leadership in ways that can be felt all across the company. Now I wish you the best of luck and offer a reminder: whenever you are feeling bogged down in a project, always remember to be Agile!

www.ingramcontent.com/pod-product-compliance
Lightning Source LLC
Chambersburg PA
CBHW051816170526
45167CB00005B/2040